THE CONFIDENT GODDESS WORKBOOK

THE CONFIDENT GODDESS WORKBOOK

CONNECTING WITH YOUR INNER POWER TO CELEBRATE THE WOMAN YOU ARE

Barbara J. Cox, Ph.D.

iUniverse, Inc.
New York Lincoln Shanghai

The Confident Goddess Workbook
Connecting with Your Inner Power to Celebrate the Woman You Are

iUniverse books may be ordered through booksellers or by contacting:

iUniverse
2021 Pine Lake Road, Suite 100
Lincoln, NE 68512
www.iuniverse.com
1-800-Authors (1-800-288-4677)

ISBN: 978-0-595-47534-6 (pbk)
ISBN: 978-0-595-91803-4 (ebk)

Printed in the United States of America

About this Workbook

This workbook is a compilation of holistic, mind-body-spirit, tools that you can use to skyrocket your self-confidence and improve your quality of life.

Goddess archetypes symbolize the traits of feminine power, confidence, and body acceptance. We can access these traits more easily in daily life by identifying with the Divine Feminine that is within each of us, and is waiting to be uncovered. My goal is to help women find ways to connect with their inner power and inner Divinity, using a variety of practical, fun and simple tools.

Self-confidence affects all facets of your life, including, career, relationships, life path, and finances. You can certainly achieve excellent results with this workbook as a self-help tool; however, you can magnify your results using this in conjunction with the Confident Goddess personalized program (See www.TheConfidentGoddess.com). Therefore, I've included pages for adding homework activities and comments that you may receive in your personalized program. I'd love to hear comments about your results and how this workbook has helped you. Feel free to email me at info@DrCoxConsulting.com.

About the Author

Barbara Cox, PhD is a holistic psychologist and transformational coach specializing in mind-body-spirit techniques that help women connect with the power to become the women they were meant to be. Her personalized sessions and workshops blend positive psychology, energy psychology, and practical spiritual tools to help you achieve your life goals more easily. With these tools, she helps you to identify and clear any blocks to your self-confidence, so that you can live the life you envision for yourself. For more information, please see her websites at www.DrCoxConsulting.com and www.TheConfidentGoddess.com.

A percentage of the profits from this book will benefit the San Diego Foundation for Change, www.foundation4change.org

Note

The information contained in this workbook is designed to help you improve self-confidence only, and not intended for the diagnosis of, prescription for, treatment of, or claims to prevent, mitigate or cure any disease, medical or psychological condition. The methods in this workbook should not be used in place of proper medical or psychological treatment. If you have any medical or mental health concerns please seek proper professional assessment and treatment.

{1}

What does confidence look like to you? In other words, what specific behaviors would you be doing daily:

Notes and Homework that I'm completing in my personalized program:

{2}

Write a note of gratitude, to yourself and to your Higher Power (whatever that represents in your belief system) for one positive quality that you have right now:

Notes and Homework that I'm completing in my personalized program:

{3}

What is one thing you can do today that would make you feel more confident? For example, you can tell yourself: "I can think of one thing I did recently where I felt confident.":

Notes and Homework that I'm completing in my personalized program:

{4} What does success look like to you? How would you describe it? Use specific events that would occur in your life or have already occurred in your life:

Notes and Homework that I'm completing in my personalized program:

{5} What is one way you can re-frame the thought, "I am not smart enough or confident enough", with a thought that is more positive and balanced? For instance, you can think of an example where you received an award or compliment for at least one talent you have. Ask your personal/executive coach or trusted friend for assistance if you need ideas:

Notes and Homework that I'm completing in my personalized program:

{6} What are 20 + positive qualities about you? Write down anything that comes to mind as you brainstorm and allow the qualities to come to you. Asked trusted friends or family for assistance if you need ideas:

Notes and Homework that I'm completing in my personalized program:

{7} Write out a script where you behave with confidence in a specific situation at work that may have been slightly uncomfortable in the past. Write the script as if it has already happened and you have become a Confident Goddess. Let your imagination soar:

Notes and Homework that I'm completing in my personalized program:

{8} Review the past 7 activities and questions and note all positive changes in your self-confidence level:

Notes and Homework that I'm completing in my personalized program:

{9}

Note one thing you are thankful for today that relates to your increased sense of self-confidence:

Notes and Homework that I'm completing in my personalized program:

{10} Find or get a picture taken of yourself where you look extra confident and joyful. Place it here as a reminder if you hit "bumpy" patches. To get a wonderful Glorious Goddess portrait taken, see: www.sacred-feminine.org.

Notes and Homework that I'm completing in my personalized program:

{11} Just for today, resist the urge to compare yourself to other women or compete with them, instead note one thing, pleasant or neutral, that you have in common with them. For example, if a high-school or college friend has a well-paying job that you are tempted to envy, instead, say to yourself, "we both are intelligent people and went to the same school.":

Notes and Homework that I'm completing in my personalized program:

{12} Here's a quick 'Releasing Blocks to Self-Confidence Meditation': Begin by sitting comfortably in a chair with your feet flat on the ground, relaxed but not slumped over, and your hands resting on your lap with your eyes closed. Bring your awareness to the base of your spine. Imagine that you are sitting outside in a natural setting on a large comfortable tree stump and that the tree roots reach all the way down to the center of the earth, connecting you with the earth; you feel a part of and connected to this tree, rooted to the earth. As you exhale, imagine that this releases any insecurities or worries about yourself down the roots of the tree and that it also allows you to release anything you want to let go of, any negative thoughts about you, any concerns, etc. As you inhale, image that the warm, golden sun is above your head, filling you up with a sense of further confidence and relaxation. You can practice this for a minute or for however long you feel inclined. What changes do you notice as you completed this meditation?

____

____

____

____

____

____

____

____

____

____

____

____

Notes and Homework that I'm completing in my personalized program:

{13}

What are you enthusiastic or passionate about currently in your life? And, how are you using this to increase your self-confidence?

Notes and Homework that I'm completing in my personalized program:

{14}

How are your inner thoughts and internal, mental dialogue growing your self-confidence? Give one example:

Notes and Homework that I'm completing in my personalized program:

{15} Write down one pleasant event that you created today and one unpleasant event that you created today and note how your actions led to that event occurring in your life. Then note one thing you learned from the 'unpleasant' event, and how you could behave differently in the future, so that you do not create that event again. This activity will increase your sense of personal power and confidence in how you can create the life you desire:

Notes and Homework that I'm completing in my personalized program:

{16} Review the past 7 activities and questions and note all positive changes in your self-confidence level:

Notes and Homework that I'm completing in my personalized program:

{17}

What is one natural talent you have that you can develop more fully in order to increase self-confidence? What is the first small step you can take to nurture that talent?

Notes and Homework that I'm completing in my personalized program:

{18}

What's one thing you can say to yourself today if you are tempted to feel insecure, in order to help yourself feel a little better? For example, you can say, "We all have up days and down days, so this will pass. I know my confidence level is building." If you are having difficulty with this, find a trusted friend or your personal/executive coach to help you devise a more helpful thought:

Notes and Homework that I'm completing in my personalized program:

{19}

What about yourself do you find interesting?

Notes and Homework that I'm completing in my personalized program:

{20}

Today, dress in an outfit or suit that makes you feel most confident. Notice how you behave more confidently:

Notes and Homework that I'm completing in my personalized program:

{21}

In what situations do you feel most authentic or comfortable and why:

Notes and Homework that I'm completing in my personalized program:

{22}

Receive a compliment by just saying 'thank you', resist any urge to deflect it. Really take in what the person said about you:

Notes and Homework that I'm completing in my personalized program:

{23} Give an authentic compliment today to someone. Make a note of one person you are grateful to have brought into your life; realize that something special about you brought that person into your life too:

Notes and Homework that I'm completing in my personalized program:

{24} Review the past 7 activities and questions and note all positive changes in your self-confidence level:

Notes and Homework that I'm completing in my personalized program:

{25}

Do one thing today, however large or small, that is out of your comfort zone, and praise yourself for doing it:

Notes and Homework that I'm completing in my personalized program:

{26} Visualize yourself as extra confident today—In order to make this even more powerful, use all of the 5 senses: What do you look like as you visualize this? How do you sound? How do you talk with others? What do others say to you as you visualize your most confident self? What cologne or scent are you wearing (it could be essential oils if you are sensitive to colognes)? What are you eating for lunch in this scenario? How do you present yourself?

Notes and Homework that I'm completing in my personalized program:

{27} As you again visualize yourself as extra confident today, add the following step: Tap, or use gentle pressure with the middle finger, on the acupressure point called the 'third eye' point; this acupressure point is located between the eyebrows, slightly above the bridge of the nose. (This point helps to maintain emotional balance.) Note any shifts or changes that occur:

Notes and Homework that I'm completing in my personalized program:

{28} If any worries or doubts appear to you as you develop your self-confidence, imagine that you sweep them out of your space, your mind-body-spirit, with a broom and that all those worries and doubts drop out of your mental space as you sweep them out. Then, fill that 'space' with one uplifting thought about yourself:

Notes and Homework that I'm completing in my personalized program:

{29} Say the statement "I enjoy who I am." What comes up when you say that? Say 'hello' to whatever feelings arise when you say the statement, acknowledge them and then let any guilt or resistance to that statement go. If you feel any residual guilt or resistance, do the following energy psychology exercise: Rub the 'sore spot' points on either side of your chest, located about 3 inches diagonal from the indent in your collarbone, while saying the following, "Even though I may have resistance or guilt when saying 'I enjoy who I am', I deeply and completely love and accept myself, honor and respect myself, and I forgive myself and anyone else who may have contributed to this guilt or resistance." Know you are a Confident Goddess!

Notes and Homework that I'm completing in my personalized program:

{30} Review the past 5 activities and questions, as well as any additional homework that you may have received, and note all positive changes in your self-confidence level:

Notes and Homework that I'm completing in my personalized program:

Great Job,
Confident Goddess!

978-0-595-47534-6
0-595-47534-5

www.ingramcontent.com/pod-product-compliance
Ingram Content Group UK Ltd.
Pitfield, Milton Keynes, MK11 3LW, UK
UKHW061830190726
13855UKWH00005B/1738